Story of St. Giles' Cathedral Church, Edinburgh. [With a plan.]

William Chambers

GUIDE TO FOLD-OUTS, MAPS and OVERSIZED IMAGES

In an online database, page images do not need to conform to the size restrictions found in a printed book. When converting these images back into a printed bound book, the page sizes are standardized in ways that maintain the detail of the original. For large images, such as fold-out maps, the original page image is split into two or more pages.

Guidelines used to determine the split of oversize pages:

• Some images are split vertically; large images require vertical and horizontal splits.
• For horizontal splits, the content is split left to right.
• For vertical splits, the content is split from top to bottom.
• For both vertical and horizontal splits, the image is processed from top left to bottom right.

STORY

OF

ST GILES' CATHEDRAL CHURCH

EDINBURGH

BY

WILLIAM CHAMBERS, LL.D.

St Giles' Cathedral Church, from the north-east.

W. & R. CHAMBERS, EDINBURGH

AND PATERNOSTER ROW, LONDON

1879

Edinburgh:
Printed by W. & R. Chambers.

STORY

OF

ST GILES' CHURCH, EDINBURGH.

ST GILES' CHURCH, Edinburgh, is the original parish church of the city. Its history can be satisfactorily traced to the early part of the twelfth century, when it superseded a church of much older date. Occupying a prominent central situation on the south side of High Street, its lofty and beautiful spire is seen from a great distance. In the course of time St Giles' has undergone various changes as regards extent and style of architecture. Externally, it seems a modern Gothic structure, with choir, nave, and transepts; but it is in reality old, of various eras, shrouded in an indifferent and comparatively recent casing. No ecclesiastical edifice in Scotland has passed through so many vicissitudes, or has been so cruelly maltreated, and yet has so tenaciously survived as an interesting memorial of the past. Identified with many stirring events in Scottish history, St Giles' may claim a national character, while it invites attention as a relic of art from the twelfth to the fifteenth century. The present brochure aspires to be only a brief historical sketch—the Story, so to speak—of this venerable edifice, along with some account of the efforts lately made towards its Restoration.

HISTORY.

As early as 854, there was a church in Edinburgh included in the list of ecclesiastical establishments belonging to the Bishopric of Lindisfarne, or Holy Island; for at that time Lothian, in which Edinburgh is situated, formed a portion of the province of Northumbria. In 1020, Earl Eadulf ceded this part of his territory to Malcolm II., king of Scotland. Whether the church in Edinburgh was at first dedicated to St Giles, is uncertain. It might have been so, for St Giles lived in the sixth century. A word may be said regarding this personage.

St Giles, or Sanctus Egidius, as he is termed in Latin, was a renowned medieval saint, of whom there are numerous legends. He is said to have been a native of Athens in Greece, and of royal lineage. From Greece he migrated to the south of France, and there in the neighbourhood of Nîmes, retired to a cave to spend his life in devotion as a hermit. The only companion of his solitude was a hind, on the milk of which animal he partly subsisted. One day, this favourite was pursued by dogs and hunters, and fled to him for protection, which it readily received. Artists have usually painted St Giles in the garb of a monk with a hind pierced by an arrow, either in his arms or at his feet. Lucas van Leyden, a Dutch painter (1494–1533), represents St Giles with an arrow piercing his hand while he is sheltering the hind; as shewn in the adjoining wood-cut. St Giles died in 541. Numerous churches and other ecclesiastical establishments, also hospitals, were founded in his honour. In England alone there were a hundred and forty-six churches dedicated to St Giles. His fame having reached Edinburgh, he was adopted as the patron saint of the church, and a

St Giles.

hind figures as one of the supporters in the city arms. For further particulars concerning 'Sanct Geill and his Hynde' we may refer to the late Mrs Jameson's tasteful work, 'Sacred and Legendary Art,' 2 vols. 1857.

A new church was erected by Alexander I. about 1120. It consisted of a choir and nave, with small side aisles and central tower, built in a massive style of the early Norman period. From all that can be learned, it covered less space than is occupied by the present edifice. It might be described as a substantial parish church, bordered by the parish burying-ground on the south, the site of which ground is now occupied by the present Parliament Square. To this St Giles' Church there are various references in old charters and other records. It is mentioned in an Act of the reign of Robert the Bruce. The circumstance of the Castle of Edinburgh having been selected as a residence by David I., is understood to have furthered the endowment and decoration of St Giles'. In 1359, David II. by a charter under the great seal 'confirmed to the chaplain officiating at the altar of St Katherine's Chapel, in the parish church of St Giles, all the lands of Upper Merchiston, the gift of Roger Hog, burgess of Edinburgh.'

The church at this early period had for its chief clergyman an official bearing the title of Vicar of St Giles, who possessed an interest in a farm called St Giles' Grange, or more familiarly Sant Geilies Grange, situated about a mile southwards, and which has communicated the name of The Grange to a pleasant suburb in this quarter. 'Under the date of 1243,' says Dr Laing, 'we find the name of a Perpetual Vicar of the Church of St Giles, Edinburgh; this circumstance, along with the earlier reference to its Grange, suggests that the church must have been attached to some religious house, and like the Priory of Coldingham, it might for a time have remained subordinate to Lindisfarne.' *

* 'The Charters of the Collegiate Church of St Giles, Edinburgh,' edited by the late Dr David-Laing. Forming one of the Bannatyne Club books, presented by Sir George Clerk, Baronet, of Penicuick, and Alexander Maconochie Welwood of Meadowbank and Garvock, Esq., the work is remarkable as a monument of Dr Laing's literary industry and antiquarian knowledge.

St Giles' Church was destined to suffer an unexpected disaster, consequent on the unhappy wars between England and Scotland in the fourteenth century.   Richard II., in retaliation for alleged wrongs, invaded Scotland with an English army in 1385.   He laid waste the country, took possession of Edinburgh, and after an occupation of five days, committed the city to the flames.   St Giles' Church perished in the conflagration.   All that remained of the building were the entrance porch, a part of the choir and nave, with the heavier portions that formed the base of the spire.

Rallying after this grievous calamity, the town was rebuilt, and the civic authorities made a strenuous effort to reconstruct St Giles'.   They entered into a contract for the building of 'five chapels' in St Giles', with pillars and vaulted roofs, covered with stone, and lighted with windows.   The contract was dated 29th November 1387, and we may assume that the reparation was completed early in the fifteenth century.   The part so executed was on the south-west of the nave.   The style of art was lighter and more ornamental than that which had been destroyed.   Afterwards, some side aisles were added through the munificence of pious individuals.   The most remarkable of these additions was the Albany Aisle, which occupies the north-west corner of the nave, and causes a projection into High Street.

In the centre of this beautiful aisle stands a light and graceful pillar, which sustains a groined roof all around. The aisle takes its name from Robert, Duke of Albany, the second son of King Robert II., who, having been intrusted with the custody of his nephew, David, Duke of Rothesay, cruelly starved him to death in a dungeon in the castle of Falkland, 1402.   Though escaping punishment for this atrocious act, Albany and his prime associate, Archibald, fourth Earl of Douglas, seem to have been haunted with a consciousness of guilt.   According to the practice of the period, they are said to have built the Albany Aisle in St Giles' as a chapel expiatory of their crime.   The capital of the pillar in the centre of the aisle bears two shields. One of these bears the Albany arms, in which the Scottish lion is quartered with the fess chequé of the Stewarts.

The other shield has the heart and other armorial bearings of the Earl of Douglas. This remarkably fine pillar, surviving as a memento of a terrible tragedy in Scottish history, and of the remorse which it occasioned, is at present almost buried

Albany Aisle.

and lost amidst the gallery and seating of the church. Our wood-engraving shews what the Albany Aisle would be if liberated.

Our historical sketch now brings us to the middle of the fifteenth century, when the renovated edifice received the addition of transepts and an extension of the choir or chancel eastwards in its present form. At the destruction of the church in 1385, three pillars on each side of the choir with the arches they supported, also part of the wall on the north side, in which were two windows, had been spared. These pillars, which are nearest the entrance, are of a plain

style, octagonal in shape, with capitals to correspond. They
bear no heraldic devices. In the course of the repairs
recently completed, when the colouring and dirt of centuries
had been removed, the marks of fire were seen on these
fine old sturdy pillars, now seven hundred years old, and
seemingly indestructible.

In the north wall, under the second window from the east,
there is a plain arched recess, the lower part being level like
a shelf. An opinion has been entertained that the recess
had formed part of a monument to Napier of Merchiston,
inventor of logarithms. This opinion is untenable. Napier
died in 1617, whereas the recess has been in the wall since
the fifteenth cen-
tury. The recess is
the relic of a mural
tomb or shrine ; the
level part having
most likely been
appropriated to a
recumbent figure.
Originally, the label
moulding on the
outer edge of the

Mural Tomb.

arch had been fringed with finely-carved crockets representing bunches of oak leaves, but these decorations were cut
away at some unknown period, to suit the plastering of the
wall ! The marks of the crockets have been traced. This
arched recess has been copied in forming a similar one on the
outer side of the wall in 1829, which contains a tablet
evidently removed from a monument of the Napier family.
The tablet is no doubt that which marked the burial-place
of the family on the south side of the church.

Passing beyond the old pillars, and approaching the great
east window, we find two pillars, one on each side, more lofty
than those of older date. They have bases of foliated sculp-
ture, fluted shafts, and elaborately ornamented capitals. Two
similar pillars are half sunk in the eastern gable. The date of
these four pillars with their lofty arches is determined by
their heraldic devices, more particularly the devices on the

first pillar on the north, usually called the King's Pillar. This pillar bears four distinct shields, which have reference to James II., king of Scotland, and his queen, Mary of Gueldres, to whom he was married in 1449. These two had a son, James, who was born in 1453. There is reason to believe that the shield facing the east, which we indicate as No. 1, was carved and set up in honour of that infant prince. It shews the Scottish lion, rampant, within a double tressure, with a label of three points, denoting an heir or prince. The shield No. 2, facing the north, impaled, and incomplete at the top, is that of the queen, Mary of Gueldres. The shield No. 3, facing the west, which has the lion, with a double tressure, also incomplete, is that of the king, James II. The shield No. 4, facing the south, has three fleurs-de-lis for France, with which country Scotland had intimate relations.

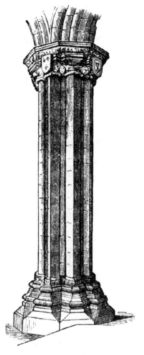

King's Pillar.

These royal shields, silent and unobtrusive, and which have happily weathered the civil and religious broils of four centuries, tell a tale of mingled joy

No. 1.   No. 2.   No. 3.

and sorrow—the birth of an heir to the throne, the death of the king, shortly followed by the death of the heart-

B

broken queen-mother. The happiness of James II. and his queen, Mary of Gueldres, was of short duration.   James, who

No. 4.

had been a kind patron of Edinburgh, was brought to it a lifeless corpse from Roxburgh, where he had been killed by the bursting of a cannon, 1460.   Mary of Gueldres, his pious widow, a patroness of art, and foundress of the Trinity College Church, survived him only three years.   Their son, the boy prince, who on the death of his father became James III., was murdered 1488.   All things considered, we are inclined to think that the date of the pillar must be set down as 1460, the imperfection in the upper part of the king and queen's shields almost pointing to the tragical event of that year.   The

No. 5.

work of reconstructing the choir went on, however, for a number of years afterwards.

On the half-pillar on the north side of the great eastern window, there is a shield, No. 5, with three cranes gorged; such being the arms of Thomas Cranstoun, a burgess and chief magistrate of Edinburgh in 1439, and again in 1454, and who most likely had taken an active part in promoting the reconstruction of the church—the city improver of his day.

We now proceed to the pillar immediately opposite, on the south side of the choir.   Here there are four shields, which we shall speak of separately.   Shield No. 6, facing the east, bears the heads of three unicorns.   Such were the Preston arms, set up in honour of William Preston of Gorton, to whom we shall immediately refer as an esteemed benefactor of the church. Shield No. 7, facing the north, bears three otter heads, being the arms of the family of Otterburn.   The person specially honoured was probably Nicholas de Otterburn, as he is styled in old writs, a learned official, much employed in public affairs, and who was Vicar of Edinburgh in 1455.   He had a nephew, John de Otterburn, who founded commemorative services in

St Giles'. Shield No. 8, facing the west, bears the arms of Kennedy, being a chevron between three crosses crossleted.

No. 6.   No. 7.   No. 8.

This is a finely executed shield, with a double tressure, and refers to a person of distinction. We have no doubt it was placed in honour of Lord James Kennedy, a grandson, of Robert III., and Bishop of St Andrews, who rendered valuable assistance to the state on the sudden death of James II., and superintended the education of James III. He was designated by Mary of Gueldres, 'our dearest cousin,' and is remembered as one of the greatest men of his time —great from being a man of learning and peaceful counsels. No 9, facing the south, is a plain shield, with a castle, the central figure in the city arms.

No. 9.

On the half-pillar next the great window on the south, is seen a shield, No. 10, bearing the arms of Napier of Merchiston, who was Lord Provost of Edinburgh in 1457. The shield, styled the Lennox shield, has a saltire, engrailed, cantoned with four rosettes, which the family of Napier assumed before the middle of the fifteenth century.

No. 10.

There are three other renderings of the city arms in the choir, but only one of them requires notice. It is a square carving in stone over the doorway to the small vestry, on the left on entering the church. As

No. 11.

shewn in the accompanying wood-cut, an angel is represented holding a shield, No. 11, on which a castle is emblazoned. This we consider to be a very old rendering, as early as the twelfth or thirteenth century. The ornamental bordering is of un-usual elegance. The existence of the stone was unknown until the recent Restoration of the choir, when by the removal of a stair, the door-way with its characteristic mould-ings was disclosed.

Besides the extension of the choir eastwards about 1460, the walls surmounting the older pillars were raised and improved. Part of the original groining which sprang from the capitals of the pillars still remains, partially chiselled away. The clerestory groining is remarkable for its rich variety of bosses. On one of the bosses is seen the monogram i h s. Around another bosse is the following legend: Ave. gra. pla. dus. tecum; such being an abbreviation of the words, *Ave Maria, gratia plena, dominus tecum* (Hail Mary, full of

mercy, the Lord be with thee). We present a wood-engraving of this remarkable bosse, which escaped erasure at the Reformation seemingly on account of its great height from the ground. It is to be viewed as an antiquarian curiosity. In the centre of some other bosses is an orifice from which had depended a chain or cord sustaining a lamp. One of these lamps had hung immediately in front of the high-altar. It is learned that the high-altar of the early church of 1120 was not shifted on the reconstruction of the choir. It remained in its original place, and there was an altar of lesser importance placed behind it, under the great eastern window.

The part of the choir between the southern row of pillars and the south wall was originally known as the Lady Aisle. Of this aisle Dr Laing says: 'In the charter dated 11th January 1454-5, it is narrated that William Preston of Gourton, then deceased, and interred in the Lady Aisle, had with diligent labour and great expense, and aided by a high and mighty prince, the king of France, and many other Lords of France, succeeded in obtaining possession of the arm-bone of St Giles; and this inestimable relique had been freely bequeathed by him "to oure mothir kirk of Sant Gell of Edynburgh withouten any condicion." The Provost, Bailies, and community of Edinburgh, deeply impressed with the importance of such an acquisition, voluntarily undertook to commence within one year, and to complete in the space of six or seven years, an aisle "furth fra our Lady Isle, where the said William lyis," to erect there his monument with a brass tablet, with his arms and an inscription, specifying his having brought that relique to Scotland; his arms also to be put in hewn stone in three other parts of the aisle; also an altar, and to endow a chaplain to sing for him from that time forth, and granting to his nearest relations the privilege of carrying the relique in all public processions.'

Such is the account given of William Preston of Gorton, whose arms, as above mentioned, consist of three heads of unicorns. The obligations in the charter were faithfully carried out. An aisle was constructed on the south, outside the Lady Aisle. For the purpose of bringing it into connection with the church, the wall, in which there were three windows, was removed; and instead of the windows, three arches were formed, with pillars corresponding to the fifteenth-century arches and pillars in the choir. A window was placed in the east end of the Preston Aisle, and three windows along its south side. The west end of the aisle opened into the south transept. The Preston Aisle was fifty-nine feet in length by twenty-four feet in breadth, by which addition the choir was considerably enlarged, while the architectural effect, enhanced by a vista of pillars, was materially improved. In the charter, a monument to Preston with a brass tablet is spoken of. It has long since disappeared.

About the time of the erection of the Preston Aisle, the ecclesiastical organisation of St Giles' underwent an important change. In 1466, a charter of James III., who was still a boy of thirteen years of age, converted the parish church of St Giles' into a collegiate foundation, with a chapter to consist of a Provost, Curate, sixteen Prebendaries, a Minister of the Choir, four Choristers, a Sacristan, and a Beadle; all of whom were exclusive of chaplains ministering at thirty-six altars throughout the establishment. Altogether, the number of ecclesiastics would not be less than a hundred, supported by particular endowments drawn from certain lands, oblations at the altars, and by donations of food and other articles. In the transition from the parochial to the collegiate organisation, William Forbes, Perpetual Vicar, was advanced to the Provostship of the new foundation. At his decease he was succeeded by Gawin Douglas, third son of Archibald, fifth Earl of Angus, and who with poetical tastes did good service to Scottish literature, which was still in its infancy. His longest poem was the 'Palace of Honour,' an apologue addressed to James IV. The most remarkable of his productions was a translation of Virgil's 'Æneid' into Scottish verse, being the first version of a Latin classic into any British tongue. Gawin Douglas was promoted to be Bishop of Dunkeld, and died in 1522.

From his literary attainments, as well as from his social position while Provost of St Giles', and as being a son of the Earl of Angus who was Lord Provost of Edinburgh, we are to imagine Gawin Douglas as a favourite guest at Holyrood, where James IV. held court with his queen, Margaret, both of whom were encouragers of learning and the useful arts. The art of printing had been introduced by Caxton into England about 1477; but it was unknown in Scotland until it was introduced by Walter Chepman and Andrew Myllar, under the auspices of James IV. and his Queen, in 1507. The types, apparatus, and workmen appear to have been brought from France. Chepman was the moneyed man in the concern, and from all we can learn, he was a person of extraordinary energy. The first work attempted was a collection of ancient ballads, forming a thin quarto volume in black-letter, which appeared in 1508. A fac-simile was reprinted in 1827, under the indefatigable editorship of Dr Laing; but copies of it are exceedingly scarce. Myllar finally gave up the printing profession, which continued to be carried on with success by Chepman, in an establishment at the head of Blackfriars Wynd, High Street. Walter Chepman became a wealthy and respected citizen, and with other properties, acquired the estate of Ewerland, near Cramond.

The wealth, piety, and munificence of Walter Chepman, the Scottish Caxton, were manifested in various endowments connected with St Giles'. On the 21st August 1513, he founded a chapel, or aisle, in honour of his royal patron and kind friend, James IV., the Queen Margaret, and their off-spring. In less than a month, James perished at Flodden, 9th of September 1513. This unfortunate event did not stop the completion of the aisle. It projected southwards from the Preston Aisle, one of the windows of which was appropriated to form the entrance, and was immediately east of the south transept, of which exteriorly it seemed an enlargement. This handsome aisle became a family chapel and place of burial. Walter Chepman died in 1532, and here he was buried.

The disturbances consequent on the change of religious sentiment in Scotland, began to break out in Edinburgh in 1556, and came to a head in 1558, when a procession of clergy on the anniversary of St Giles, 1st September, was riotously dispersed by the populace. An effigy of the saint was torn in pieces; and soon afterwards, in the national convulsion, the clerical community of this ancient church disappear, while their means of livelihood are confiscated. As concerns the deplenishing of the church, the civic authorities inter-fered. By the help of sailors from Leith, with ropes and ladders, the altars were taken down, and cleared out. All the gold, silver, and other valuables were carefully catalogued and secured, as may be seen from existing town records. After being stripped of its silver mountings, the arm-bone of St Giles, which about a hundred years previously had been thought so very precious, was, as is alleged, thrown into the adjacent burying-ground. It was a clean sweep.

Excepting perhaps a pulpit or a reading-desk, and a few benches, nothing was left in the old edifice.

Under the settlement of affairs at the Reformation, 1560, the collegiate character of St Giles' Church disappeared, and it resumed its original condition of a parish church. John Knox was constituted pastor, with a suitable stipend from the city funds. In starting afresh after the recent clearing out, the church must have presented an empty desolate appearance. At that period there were no fixed pews. The seats were chairs or wooden stools, provided chiefly by worshippers for their own accommodation. The bulk of the people stood, and they would gladly stand for hours listening to their favourite preacher. John Knox often preached, it is said, to three thousand persons. The work he went through was immense. He preached twice on Sunday, and three times every other day of the week, besides attending to other clerical duties. His only assistant was a 'Reader.' The choir of the church with its extensions on the south we have referred to, formed the place of assemblage; but the voice of the preacher rang through the nave and far withdrawing aisles, which were left open, and formed a convenient lounge for the citizens. That is the picture we are to form of the interior of St Giles' Church immediately after the Reformation.

Knox occupied a conspicuous position when acting as chaplain at the funeral of the 'Good Regent,' James Stewart, Earl of Murray, who was assassinated at Linlithgow, 23d January 1569-70. The occasion is memorable in the history of St Giles'. 'Upon Tuesday, the 14th of February,' says M'Crie, 'the Regent's corpse was brought from the palace of Holyrood, and interred in the south aisle of the collegiate Church of St Giles'. Before the funeral, Knox preached a sermon on these words: "Blessed are the dead who die in the Lord." Three thousand persons were dissolved in tears before him while he described the Regent's virtues and bewailed his loss. Buchanan paid his tribute to the memory of the deceased by writing the inscription placed on his monument with that impressive simplicity and brevity which are dictated by genuine grief.'

The death of Murray led to a keen contest as to who should be Regent. The choice fell on the Earl of Lennox, paternal grandfather of the young king, James VI. This gave offence to Sir William Kirkaldy of Grange, who had hitherto belonged to the king's party, and as such was Governor of Edinburgh Castle. He now changed sides, went over to the party of the exiled Mary Queen of Scots, and commenced a fierce civil war, in which he fortified Edinburgh, and on the 28th March 1571, placed a military force on the roof and steeple of St Giles' Church, to keep the citizens in awe. The craftsmen of the city, however, were not easily daunted. They broke into the church, and to bring matters to a crisis, proposed to pull down the pillars which sustained the roof. Alarmed for their safety, Kirkaldy's men, on the 4th June, began to make holes in the vaulted ceiling, from which they fired down with muskets on the crowd of assailants. Calderwood, the church historian, says they 'made the vaute like a riddle to shoot through;' which gives us an impressive idea of this warlike strife inside a church. Kirkaldy withdrew his forces in July 1572. Under the merciless Regency of Morton, he was hanged at the Cross of Edinburgh, 3d August 1573.

The roof of the church being duly repaired after the late hostile visitation, things went on in their usual quiet way. But St Giles' was destined to suffer infinitely more damage than anything that had been done to it by the operations of Kirkaldy of Grange—damage that has taken three centuries to remedy, and is not remedied yet. Previous to the death of Knox, the magistrates and council began to section the church of St Giles' into separate divisions. This proceeding was commenced within ten years after the Reformation. The first division we hear of was the Tolbooth Church, situated at the south-west corner of the edifice. 'On Sunday, 21st September 1572,' says M'Crie, 'Knox began to preach in the Tolbooth Church, which had been fitted up for him.' On Sunday, 9th November following, he preached in the same place at the installation of Lawson, his colleague and successor. 'After the sermon,' adds M'Crie, 'he removed with the audience to the larger church,' that is, to the choir, which luckily escaped sectionising. This was John Knox's last sermon. On quitting the church leaning feebly on his staff, he was attended down the street to his house by his audience, to take the last look of their pastor. He died on the 24th November, and was buried in the churchyard of St Giles'. The spot cannot now be identified. It is near to the equestrian statue of Charles II. in the Parliament Square.

In May 1590, James VI. and his young queen, Anne of Denmark, ceremoniously visited St Giles' Church, when there were thanksgivings for their marriage and safe arrival in Scotland. The choir, which was fitted up for the occasion, henceforth became a place of public worship for the king and queen, and from this time we begin to hear of a royal pew, or 'loft,' with seats for the officers of state, the judges, and the magistrates of the city. James sometimes went to St Giles' for the purpose of delivering public orations; he did so on Sunday, 3d April 1603, to bid farewell to the citizens on his departure to take possession of the throne of England.

An overturn now ensues in the ecclesiastical character of St Giles', consequent on the introduction of Laud's Service-book into Scotland, by Charles I. Edinburgh was erected into a bishopric, 29th September 1633, and an order was given to the magistrates and council to convert St Giles' into a cathedral church. The choir of the cathedral church of Durham was pointed out as a model. The tumult that took place on the attempt to introduce the Service-book, Sunday, 23d July 1637, along with subsequent events, restored the church for the Presbyterian form of worship. The scene of the tumult, where Jenny Geddes threw a stool at the head of the Dean of Edinburgh, was in the south transept, or Middle Church, as some historians call it; the choir at the time being in course of preparation for the cathedral service. Consequent on the tumult and the circumstances that ensued, St Giles' ceased to have the status of a cathedral; but this was resumed on the establishment of Episcopacy in 1662. It remained so until the Revolution of 1688, when Alexander Rose, the last of the race of prelates, was ejected. The building is still popularly designated St Giles' Cathedral, or St Giles' Cathedral Church.

Besides the choir, which formed the parish church, there was at first only the Tolbooth Church, as a subordinate place of worship in St Giles'. In the other parts of the building there were accommodated, under varying conditions, a grammar-school, courts of justice, a town-clerk's office, a prison, and a weaver's workshop. In an odd corner was kept the apparatus for public executions. It was a queer jumble, designed to meet public wants, with little regard to congruity. St Giles', however, in the palmiest of its pre-Reformation days, had a certain dash of secularism in its spiritual character. From the want of a place of public resort for men of business, the church offered a means of meeting to persons who had to enter into or discharge contracts, to pay accounts, and so forth; for which miscellaneous purposes the high-altar of St Giles', or some other altar in the church, was a stipulated place of meeting. In such acts of desecration, one is in a small way reminded of the practices which were so objectionable in the Temple of Jerusalem.

After the clearance at the Reformation, St Giles' was still haunted for business transactions. The south transept became the favourite resort; and when the Earl of Murray's monumental tomb was set up, it answered as well as the old high-altar at which to make bargains or to discharge obligations. From a popular belief that Duke Humphry of Gloucester, youngest son of Henry IV., was buried in Old St Paul's, there arose the jocularity that persons who strolled about in St Paul's for want of a dinner, were said to dine with Duke Humphry. A similar pleasantry prevailed concerning the tomb of the Earl of Murray. Sempill, a Scottish poet, refers in verse to the spot as a convenient lounge for impecunious and hungry idlers. One of them with sad internal commotion pathetically says:

> 'I dined with saints and gentlemen,
>   Ev'n sweet Saint Giles and the Earl of Murray.'

Long before the Reformation, St Giles' had been freely used as a place of interment. In most cases the interments were in graves below the floor, as was not unusual in old edifices of this kind, and is still in a limited way the case in

Westminster Abbey. Persons of distinction were entombed in one or more vaults in the southern aisles. Here the Earl of Murray, as above related, was interred in 1569–70; his representative is the present Earl of Moray. The next individual of note laid in this quarter was John Stewart, fourth Earl of Athole, Lord High Chancellor of Scotland, who died in 1579. His title was conferred on John Murray, Earl of Tullibardine, who married his grand-daughter. The representative of the family is now the Duke of Athole. A third distinguished person entombed near the spot was John Graham, third Earl of Montrose, High Treasurer, and afterwards Lord High Chancellor. On the accession of James VI. to the throne of England, he was appointed Viceroy in Scotland, presided at the parliament at Perth, 1606, and died in 1608.

The grandson of this last-mentioned personage was James Graham, fifth Earl, created Marquis of Montrose, who distinguished himself as a military commander in the cause of Royalty during the Civil War. Montrose's history is well known. Captured and brought into Edinburgh, he was condemned, and executed 21st May 1650. His body was dismembered. His limbs were sent to different parts of Scotland, while his head was stuck on a pike on the Tolbooth. After the Restoration, the scattered remains were collected with tokens of respect, and deposited in the Abbey of Holyrood. Thence they were brought by a solemn funeral procession, at which the magistrates of Edinburgh assisted, and entombed in St Giles', 14th May 1661. The ordinary opinion is that his tomb was in the aisle of Walter Chepman. Mark Napier, in his Memoirs of Montrose, states that he was interred in the vault of his grandfather, the Viceroy of Scotland. This doubtful point afterwards receives consideration. The descendant and representative of the Marquis is the present Duke of Montrose. The burial of persons of note in St Giles' did not cease till past the middle of the eighteenth century.

In process of time, as Edinburgh grew in population, more parish churches were required. The proper course would have been to build new churches within the parishes to which they nominally pertained. Instead of this, a plan was adopted of utilising St Giles', by cutting it up into sections, and calling each section a parish church. Hence, the grouping of churches for different congregations in this unfortunate building. The grammar-school, the courts of justice, the town-clerk's office, the weaver's workshop, and the machinery of the gallows got edged out, and the general aspect of affairs was more spiritualised, though not a little repugnant to the senses. At the middle of the eighteenth century, the list of churches in the edifice stood as follows. The Choir or High Church in the east; the Tolbooth Church in the south-west; Haddo's Hole Church in the north-west; and the Old Church in the middle and part of the south side. This allocation left two portions of the building undisposed of. These were the Preston Aisle, which was used for meetings of various kinds; and the dark central space under the spire with the north transept. This last-mentioned portion was finally fitted up as the Police Office. We remember St Giles' in this condition in 1818.

What will strike every one with surprise is, that throughout the eighteenth and the early years of the present century there should have been such a general acquiescence in the odious internal condition of St Giles' Church. Arnot, the historian of Edinburgh, who wrote in 1779, and gives a list of the congregations which then confusedly nestled in the building, and must have suffered from the mass of decaying mortality beneath their feet, has not a word of remonstrance on the subject. There were accomplished men of letters in Edinburgh at a still later period who are now reckoned among national luminaries. Not one of them, as far as we know, imagined there was anything wrong in the unseemly state of St Giles'. They complacently saw before their eyes an edifice abounding in some of the finest specimens of fifteenth-century architecture degraded into a collection of wretchedly fetid caverns. But the same dearth of taste as regards ecclesiastical structures and the comfort of congregations prevailed almost everywhere until very recent times.

Before it was despoiled, 1558-60, the vast interior of this grand old building, with its many pillars and groined roof, must have presented an appearance resembling that of a

spacious English cathedral of the olden class. The policy of
cutting up and apportioning this handsome structure, on
which so much architectural taste had been lavished, is inex-
cusable. The transformation was effected in a manner altogether tasteless. No care was taken to preserve the finer parts
of the architecture. Rows of fluted pillars sustaining lofty
arches were merged in the rough walls which were erected
length-wise and crosswise to form the several compartments.
The foliated bases and capitals of pillars were hacked without
mercy to bring them within the required line. Characteristic
heads carved among the foliage were knocked off with
hammers, and are found buried in rubbish beneath the floor.
The erection of galleries in all the churches caused further

Norman Porch.

dilapidation, as cavities for beams to sustain these galleries
were dug in the sides of several pillars.

It has been stated that the ancient entrance-porch was among the parts spared at the conflagration of 1385. This porch was on the north side of the building, and was connected with the nave, so as to form a convenient entrance from the public thoroughfare. The arch, rounded in form, was of an ornate Norman style. The archivolt in several divisions exhibited figures of animals and grotesque heads, along with crenellated and chevron mouldings. By an act of barbarism, this ancient arch, a precious relic of the twelfth century, was taken down and utterly destroyed in the course of some repairs on the building in 1797 or 1798. Fortunately, before its removal, a representation of it was taken by an artist, of which an engraved copy appears as a frontispiece to Dr Laing's laborious work on St Giles'.

Under the authority of successive acts of parliament, the municipality of Edinburgh was extended, and churches for new parochial divisions were erected in various places at considerable cost to the civic corporation. Nevertheless, St Giles' remained in the condition now described until the first quarter of the nineteenth century. There were still four churches and a Police Office under one roof. In 1817, by the removal of small shops or 'krames,' which had long existed within the niches of the ancient building, the exterior had a very ragged appearance. Public sentiment was roused. Something must be done to renovate St Giles'. For several years the subject received the consideration of the Town Council, and a plan for remodelling the church, by Mr Burn, architect, was at length adopted. The cost was to be about £20,000, towards which sum government contributed £12,600. Dr Laing gives an excellent ground-plan of St Giles', before it was touched by Mr Burn; but by a singular mistake of the artist in framing the scale of feet, the building is represented as being about two hundred and fifty feet long. Its true measurement was a hundred and ninety-six feet in length within the walls, by a hundred and thirty feet wide at the transepts. The ground plan we offer as a frontispiece shews its present dimensions and character.

Burn commenced his operations in 1829, and the work was finished in 1833. Two aisles on the north side were taken

away.   On the south-west, two of the 'five chapels' or aisles,
contracted for in 1387, were removed, while other alterations
were made in this part of the building.   Picturesque roofs
and pinnacles disappeared.   The whole fabric was new
cased in a bald style of art.   As concerns the interior,
the sectioning into parts was only modified.   The choir
remained as before.   The southern section of the building
was fitted up for meetings of the General Assembly; but
this appropriation not being found satisfactory, the Old
Church in a few years afterwards here took up its quarters.
The best thing done was the expulsion of the Police Office.
For it, was substituted a capacious lobby, common to the
several congregations, who all entered by one outer door
in the north transept.   There was an alteration of names.
The Tolbooth Church and Haddo's Hole statutorily vanish.
The nave is occupied by the New North Church, now
designated West St Giles'.   It is much to be deplored that,
in the course of this remodelling, the fine old monument
of the Earl of Murray, which had once been a place of
resort, and was otherwise interesting, was destroyed.   'It
might have been thought,' says Dr Laing, 'that such a
monument would have escaped any sacrilegious hand; but
to the disgrace of our civic authorities, it was allowed to
be demolished, and the brass tablet, containing engraved
figures of Justice and Faith, with an inscription written by
Buchanan, was removed.'   The brass tablet, however, was not
lost.   As after described, it is to be seen on the modern
monument of the Earl of Murray.

So much for Mr Burn's improvements on St Giles'.   By
some, they are thought to have made matters worse rather
than better.   Fortunately, the spire of St Giles' escaped his
attentions.   This spire, as will be seen by our vignette in
title-page, is a handsome square structure, terminating in
decorated arches and pinnacles, producing the appearance of
an imperial crown, and rising to a height of a hundred and
sixty-one feet.   It is of old date, but underwent repair
without damage to its appearance in 1648.   Towering over
the centre of the Old Town, it is visible for many miles
distant.

RESTORATIONS.

When the present writer had the honour of being Lord Provost of Edinburgh, 1865-69, he had often occasion to attend public worship officially with the other magistrates and members of the Town Council. The place of assemblage was the choir, or High Church, in the front of a gallery on the north side, having the King's Pillar on the right, and the half-pillar with the Cranston arms on the left. In the corresponding gallery on the south were the seats for the judges of the Supreme Court of Scotland. Intermediately, in front of the great east window, was a huge dark pulpit, with a lofty sounding-board; such being the pulpit from which Hugh Blair delivered his admired sermons a hundred years ago. At the west end of the church was the gallery with the Royal pew. It was a homely structure, consisting of a light blue-painted canopy, supported by four wooden posts, over a few tawdry arm-chairs. The technical name of this kind of structure is a baldachino. No one could look at it without being reminded of a four-post bed. Here George IV. was seated when he attended church on his visit to Edinburgh, 1822; and here for two Sundays every year sat the Lord High Commissioner to the General Assembly. The whole seating of the church was of plain deal. A cram of old-fashioned pews from floor to ceiling. There was a distressing mustiness in the atmosphere, which ventilation failed to remedy, for the ground was saturated with human remains, which ought long since to have been removed as dangerous to the health of the congregation.

There and then, when seated in that elevated gallery close to the carved shields of the boy-prince James and his mother the inestimable Mary of Gueldres, we conceived the idea of attempting a restoration of the building, and producing a church in which the people of Edinburgh might feel some pride—a shrine fitting for the devotional exercises of Royalty. It would cost some trouble. But what good thing is ever done without trouble? There would be no harm in trying. Shortly afterwards, we called a meeting to take the matter into consideration, 1st November 1867.   The scheme was generally approved; but difficulties interposed, and it was laid aside until 1871, when with recovered health and more leisure, it could be prosecuted with a better chance of success. At a public meeting, a Restoration Committee was appointed, with the present writer as Chairman.   The object of the Committee was eventually to restore as far as practicable the whole interior of St Giles', but to effect this step by step as circumstances permitted, and to confine operations in the first place to the choir.   The idea of thoroughly restoring an edifice so damaged by alterations was hopeless.   But much might be done.   The intervening walls could be taken down. The pillars might be mended.   With patience, the outlay of money, and the concurrence of the civic and ecclesiastical authorities, the building could probably be brought back to something like what it had been in long-past times.

The efforts to gather subscriptions for the object in view were at first as successful as could be expected.   Her Majesty the Queen headed the list with a subscription of £200.   The Town Council of Edinburgh, the Royal College of Surgeons, the Societies of High Constables of Edinburgh and Holyrood, and the Society of Writers to the Signet, were among the public bodies who subscribed liberally.   Nobility and gentry of all denominations contributed to facilitate an object which was felt to be national in its character.   In June 1872, when the amount of subscriptions had reached £2000, the Committee, with consent of the authorities concerned, felt warranted in commencing the work.   The galleries which disfigured the building were wholly removed, thereby developing the fine old pillars, which were mended with stone to resemble the original.   The baldachino and the furniture of the Royal pew were taken away as crown property.   All the pews and the pulpit were removed.   When everything was gone, the floor was trenched throughout to a depth of several feet. No vaults were discovered, but there was an immense quantity of human remains, which were taken away in hearses and decently buried in a churchyard.   A number of large grave-stones were removed that had served as pavement, on which the professional devices of craftsmen were rudely carved. These slabs were put at the disposal of a corporate body representing the craftsmen of Edinburgh. As a final act, the walls and groined roof of the choir were cleaned, and rendered pleasing to the eye.

Under direction of Mr W. Hay, architect, the process of renewal according to the best style of art, was now commenced. The passages were laid with Minton tiles bearing antique Scottish devices. A pulpit of Caen stone exquisitely

Pulpit.

carved by Mr John Rhind, an Edinburgh sculptor, was placed against the pillar on the south side nearest the east window. All the seatings were of oak. The seats for the magistrates and for the judges bore appropriate carvings. The Royal pew at the west end, raised above the general level, was a highly ornamental structure, with suitable devices. The cost of the Government pews, including the Royal pew, and pews for the judges, alone cost £1586, towards which the Treasury reluctantly made a grant of £500. Altogether

Royal Pew.

the cost of restoring the choir, as now described, including the expense of heating by hot-water pipes, amounted to £4490. The subscriptions actually realised fell short of that sum to the extent of £650, which deficiency was made good by the Chairman and several members of Committee. Thus the transaction was closed. Throughout the whole affair, the Committee owed much to the valuable services of Mr Lindsay Mackersey, W.S., Honorary Secretary.

According to appointment, the choir, in its renovated form, was opened for public worship on Sunday, 9th March 1873. From the interest taken in the alterations, the church was crowded. At the morning and afternoon services, the judges, magistrates, and various public bodies attended in official costume, the spectacle being peculiarly effective. Latterly, under the incumbency of the Rev. Dr J. Cameron Lees, the church in its improved form has become one of the most attractive in Edinburgh.

The second step taken in the process of restoration was as follows: The southern section of St Giles', embracing the Preston Aisle and other parts already mentioned, had been used as the Old Church, with windows overlooking the Parliament Square. By an Act of Parliament, 1870, the Old Church parish was dropped out of the statutory parochial divisions. The church was occupied for a time on a temporary footing, and at length disused. Such was the state of matters in 1878, and an opportunity was afforded of clearing out and restoring this portion of the building. Plans were prepared by Mr W. Hay, and approved by the Restoration Committee. The estimated cost was £1500. The plans being submitted to the Ecclesiastical Commissioners and the Magistrates and Council, received their approval, but only under a guarantee given by the present writer that he would be responsible for the expense of the undertaking. As to the guarantee, it will be duly liquidated without troubling any one for subscriptions.

In February 1879, the work of restoration began by removing the galleries and pews, taking down partitions and staircases, lifting the floor, and opening up the aisles. By the lifting of the floor, a hideous scene of decaying mortal remains was disclosed. Thickly beneath the floor lay heaps of skulls and bones in indiscriminate confusion, like the emptyings of a churchyard. The whole of the bones that were collected might probably weigh two tons. In a number of cases the remains had belonged to persons buried in the spot, but by far the larger proportion consisted of clearings from parts of the building removed or altered by Mr Burn, who at first, as a ready means of disposal, carted loads of bones to a 'Dry toom,' a term equivalent to 'Dry rubbish may be shot here.' This did not answer. The spectacle of skulls rolling like turnips down a bank of rubbish, and settling in ghastly rows at the foot, went beyond public endurance. On some complaint being made, the carting was stopped, and the less costly device was resorted to of spreading the mortal remains under the floor of what was designed to be a place of meeting for the General Assembly, and which was afterwards the Old Church. In whatever manner they came there, all the bones were now collected into large boxes, to await an examination by anatomists previous to removal to a burying-ground. In the soil of the Preston Aisle, about a foot below the surface, was found a leaden coffin, bearing the inscription, 'Brigadier Richart Cunyngham, Died 26th Nov. 1697, Ætat 47.' The Brigadier had probably been a connection of the Dick-Cunynghams, baronets, of Prestonfield. The coffin was in an imperfect condition, and has been left undisturbed.

After a general clearance, the first operations were directed to the aisle founded by Chepman, and which is sometimes called the Montrose Aisle, from a belief that the Marquis of Montrose had been here entombed. This once elegant aisle was in a revolting condition. The arch between it and the Preston Aisle had been built up. It was divided into three floors. The lower floor was degraded into a coal-cellar; in the middle floor was placed a tall iron stove for heating by means of flues; and the upper floor formed an apartment, with a fire-place and other accessories. The floors were taken down, and the whole interior cleared out. It was expected that the remains of Montrose would be found in the coal-cellar; but nothing of the kind was discovered. The ground was trenched, but still no appearance of relics of the Great Marquis. Had they been recklessly dug out and thrown away at the time of Burn's remodelling of St Giles', or had they never been there at all, but were interred in an adjoining vault? This doubtful point was left to be cleared up by future explorations. Only two or three fragments of leg-bones were found in the soil, as if left by accident. Anatomists pronounced them to be the bones of a person from fifty to sixty years of age. They could not therefore belong to Montrose, who died at the age of thirty-eight. They may have belonged to Chepman, and have been returned to the soil.

When the thick wall that blocked up Chepman's Aisle was removed, the fluted jambs sustaining the arch were found to be much shattered. About twelve feet of the jambs on each side had been cut away. A chimney had been run right through the key-stone of the arch. The whole was repaired by inserting fresh hewn stone to resemble the original. The result has been a handsome arch in the style of the fifteenth century. The lath and plaster which had been stuck on the walls of the aisle were wholly removed, and the original character of the stone-work was developed. A floor supported on brick arches over a vault completed the restoration.

In the process of cleaning the groined roof of the aisle, which was begrimed with dirt and coatings of whitewash, a finely carved bosse was discovered, bearing the arms of Walter Chepman impaled with those of his first wife, who had belonged to the family of Kerkettill. The joint arms are on a shield held up by an angel. A corbel which terminated the groining of the roof on the west side bore a pious symbolic carving. It represents an eagle, the

Chepman's Arms.

emblem of St John the Evangelist; the eagle, in sacred and legendary art, being the symbol of the highest inspiration, because St John soared upwards to the contemplation of the divine nature of the Saviour. Close to the eagle is a scroll legend in black-letter, *In principio,* being the two words with which the gospel of St John in the Latin Vulgate begins—*In principio erat Verbum :* ' In the beginning was the Word.' According to the charter of endowment, Chepman dedicated the altar in his chapel to St John, whom he had pro-

Emblem of St John.

bably adopted as his patron saint. The disclosing of these old carvings adds to the archæological interest in St Giles'.

It has been thought that as something is due to Chepman for his service to literature, it would only be becoming to set up a tablet with a suitable inscription to his memory. A tablet accordingly is now in preparation to be placed in his aisle, bearing the following inscription: 'To the Memory of Walter Chepman, designated the Scottish Caxton, who under the auspices of James IV. and his Queen Margaret, introduced the art of Printing into Scotland 1507; founded this aisle in honour of the King and Queen and their family 1513; and died in 1532; this Tablet is gratefully inscribed by William Chambers, LL.D., 1879.'

Repairs on the Preston Aisle are being proceeded with in order that it may be re-united to the choir previous to November in the present year. These repairs involve the

Baptismal Font.

mending of the pillars and arches which have been seriously damaged by the insertion of beams and otherwise. In some instances the bases and the ornamental capitals of the pillars have had to be replaced. On the re-union with the choir a considerable addition will be made in the accommodation for worshippers. Through the munificence of a friend of the Rev. Dr J. C. Lees, the church will at the same time receive the addition of a baptismal font in Caen stone, executed by Mr Rhind, on the model of Thorwaldsen's famous work at Copenhagen. It represents an angel wreathed with flowers, kneeling on one knee, holding a large shell, intended to contain the water for baptism. The font will be placed at the opening of the eastern arch from the Preston Aisle.

As preparatory to restoring the south transept, it was necessary to make some excavations, by which it was hoped a discovery would be made of certain vaults that were believed to be in this part of the building. A search for these vaults took place on the 10th April, when only one vault was discovered. It was close to the west wall of the transept, and near the spot on which had stood the Regent Murray's tomb. The vault measured about sixteen feet long by little more than three feet wide. In it were three leaden coffins, in a bad condition. The most perfect of these leaden coffins, as seen by the arms and inscriptions, contained the remains of Alexander, fourth Earl of Galloway, born 1670, died 1690. The other two leaden coffins bore neither arms nor inscriptions, and seemed to pertain to persons of a slight figure. It was the opinion of a medical authority present that the remains in one of the coffins were those of a young man; and that the remains in the other were those of a female of middle age. Near these leaden coffins was found a leaden plate, bearing the engraved inscription, 'Francis Steuart, Esq., died at Rheims in France, 7th Octr. 1768, Aged 22.' The plate had probably been on a wooden coffin that lay in fragments, and in which the leaden coffin had been placed. The Francis Steuart referred to was a son of the Hon. Francis Steuart of Pittendriech, third son of Francis, sixth Earl of Moray.

A quantity of skulls and bones were found in the vault. All were carefully replaced alongside the leaden coffins, and to prevent intrusion, the vault was immediately built up. The examination satisfied every one that the remains of the Regent Murray, the Earl of Athole, the Earl of Montrose, the Marquis of Montrose, and Napier of Merchiston, all said to have been entombed in vaults in this quarter, were not to be found. There was no vault but that which contained the coffins above mentioned. Eastward from that vault, within the compass of the south transept, there were two inclosures

formed by dwarf walls, that might at one time have been
vaults. On lifting the flags that covered these inclosures,
they were found to contain rubbish, with which a few bones
of no significance were mingled. There was likewise found
a quadrangular built pit in the floor of the church, that
might originally have been a vault. Like the others, it
was filled with rubbish and bones. If these various inclosures
had really been vaults, their proper contents had been removed,
no one knows whither, in the course of alterations on this
part of the building, 1829 to 1833, at which time the ancient
and historical tomb of the Earl of Murray was destroyed.

In the Edinburgh newspapers under date January 23, 1830,
there occurs a notice of the alterations then taking place in
St Giles', in which it is stated that on the removal of the
tomb of the Regent Murray, the contents were transferred to
another vault previously prepared immediately to the east of
the old one, in which were three leaden coffins. There is
here some inaccuracy. As has just been seen, the leaden
coffins are in a vault close to the west wall of the transept,
and could not be *east* of the spot on which had stood the
Regent Murray's tomb. As to this vault being *previously*
prepared, it had existed at least since 1690, when it received
the body of Alexander, fourth Earl of Galloway. We have
mentioned that the contents of the inclosures or vaults
on the east were chiefly rubbish. It comes to this: The
remains of the Regent Murray are either in the form of
loose bones in the vault we have described, or they were
intermingled with the mass of mortal remains that were
treated so unceremoniously by Mr Burn, and a residue of
which now awaits examination by anatomists. A special
object in this examination is, if possible, to find some relics
of the Marquis of Montrose. As his legs and arms were
rudely severed on the scaffold, there is a faint hope that by
such tokens of mutilation they may be identified. To think
that through reckless mismanagement, this is the last chance
of discovering the bones of the Great Marquis!

These explanations are offered with a view to rectify some
erroneous notions that seem to be entertained respecting the
extent of the late discoveries in St Giles'. The state of

matters is precisely as now related. The strange disappearance of the remains of illustrious dead from the spot in which by history and tradition they are said to have been placed, raises a painful reflection regarding the indifference to matters of this kind so lately as half a century ago. Only now, in 1879, has the disappearance of the remains become known. Should any fresh discovery be made, which is not likely, it will be duly announced.

In fitting up the south transept, care will be taken of the modern monument of the Regent Murray already referred to. It is a tasteful wall structure of Caen stone, erected by the late John, eleventh Earl of Moray, 1864. Near the top is placed the old brass tablet, which, besides the arms of the Regent, with the motto—SALUS PER CHRISTUM (Salvation through Christ), bears on one side an emblematic figure of Faith or Piety, with the words PIETAS SINE VINDICE LUGET (Piety mourns without defence), on the other side a figure of Justice, with the words JUS EXARMATUM EST (Justice has been disarmed). Date beneath, 23 Januarii 1569, followed by Buchanan's admired Latin inscription: 'JACOBO STOVARTO MORAVIÆ COMITI SCOTIÆ PROREGI VIRO ÆTATIS SUÆ LONGE OPTIMO AB INIMICIS OMNIS MEMORIÆ DETERRIMIS EX INSIDIIS EXTINCTO CEU PATRI COMMUNI PATRIA MŒRENS POSUIT.' Translation: 'To James Stewart, Earl of Moray, Regent of Scotland, a man by far the noblest of his time, barbarously slain by enemies, the vilest in history; his country mourning has raised this monument as to a common father.'

The last thing to be done will be the restoration of the aisle immediately west of the south transept. This aisle consisted originally of two arches, sustained on a single pillar on the side towards the church. Mr Burn reduced the aisle one half. He took away the western part, removed the single sustaining pillar, and built up the gap with a blank wall. The aisle was now a square inclosure appropriated as a staircase with a side entrance. In these operations a fine work of art was fortunately spared, though removed eastwards, and placed immediately under the remaining window. It is a tolerably complete relic of a mural tomb or shrine, dedicated to the Passion of Christ. Like the similar

but less ornamental relic of art in the choir, it consists
of a Gothic arch over a level slab, on which possibly
there had been a recumbent figure. The emblematic
carvings are profuse and minute. They embody repre-
sentations of the crown of thorns, the scourge, the nails,

Mural Tomb or Shrine.

the sponge, and other symbols of the Passion. The restoration of the aisle to its former dimensions and character
is impracticable. All that can be done is to clear out the
staircase, which is no longer required, and to substitute for
the blank wall towards the church a Gothic arch with jambs,
which will bring the mural tomb fully into view.

Here we meanwhile close our narrative. From the activity
with which operations are carried on, it is expected that the
restoration of the southern section of the building will be
completed early in 1880. In other words, there will be a
clear sweep of paved flooring a hundred and twenty-two
feet in length, by twenty-four feet in breadth, exclusive of
side aisles, the whole with a lofty groined roof overhead.

Thus, two-thirds of this venerable edifice will have been restored. The nave, occupied by the congregation of West St Giles', will then alone remain in an objectionable condition. The Restoration Committee unite in a generally expressed desire that the nave should be cleared out in the same manner as the other portions of the building. Were this effected, some valuable specimens of fourteenth and fifteenth century art would be disclosed, including the Albany Aisle, of which there is an illustration in a previous page. Looking to the immense quantity of decaying mortal remains found underneath the flooring of the choir and aisles, it is not unreasonable to conclude that a like state of things prevails in connection with the nave, which cannot be too speedily remedied. Of course, nothing can be done unless a church be provided elsewhere permanently for the congregation; but this is a matter which does not pertain to the Restoration Committee. It is enough for the present writer to say that if the nave be delivered over in the same confiding spirit as the choir and aisles, he has offered to be at the entire expense that may be required for its restoration—only stipulating that the offer, which is addressed to the public authorities concerned, must be either accepted or rejected by Whitsunday 1880. Besides being of service to the historian and to the student of architecture, the opening up of the whole of St Giles', so as to develop the characteristic beauty of this grand old ecclesiastical structure, is felt to be of that National import which invites general co-operation and sympathy. Independently of other considerations, the entire restoration of the building would certainly add one more to the many attractions of EDINBURGH.

CPSIA information can be obtained
at www.ICGtesting.com
Printed in the USA
BVHW022359271222
655118BV00004B/20